How to Start and Own Your WordPress Blog ~ Made Easy

by Ferd Crotte

Contents

Title

Copyright

Contents

Introduction

Envision Your Blog

The Title and Tagline

Choosing a Blogging Platform

Hosted vs Self Hosted Blogs

Create Your Blog!

Themes

Your First Post

Comments

Finding Interested Readers

Editing and Deleting

Adding Pictures to Your Posts

More About Images

Plugins and Widgets

RSS Feeds

Statistics

Adding HTML Code to Widgets

Final Thoughts and Credits

About the Author

Introduction

A blog is a web site that anyone can create for personal use. It is a very popular way for people to publish their thoughts and ideas on the World Wide Web and to find an audience of interested readers.

Since you are reading this book, you are probably interested in the world of blogging, and maybe thinking of starting your own blog. This book will help you do just that! I'll assume that you know absolutely nothing about how to do it. Of course, if you already have some knowledge you can skip over the areas with which you are familiar and concentrate on what is new.

I want to start a blog! :-)

The word "blog" is short for "web log." This refers to anything that is written (a "log") on the World Wide Web. Web log. We**blog**. Blog. The word "blog" can refer to a single written article (a post) or to your entire web site. It can also be used a a verb, "to blog" (to write on your blog) about something. A web site referred to as a blog is usually written by an individual or by a small group of collaborators. It usually has a vision or a purpose, and in this there is a huge variety. At the last count in 2012, there were 182 million blogs on the Internet, as tracked by BlogPulse. Let's call those 182 million blogs the "blogosphere!" On the blogosphere, one can find a blog on any particular subject, and personal blogs which are more like public diaries, and anything in between. Blog writers want their blog to be read by as many people as possible. A blog usually has a way for a reader to write a comment in response to what has been written. Reader/commenters usually return to blogs that catch their interest. A relationship between the writer and the reader/commenter then develops. In this way, blogs create communities of like-minded people who may be physically scattered all over the world. That sense of community is the heart and soul of blogging!

Throughout this book, I will use my own personal blog as an example. If you have never visited a blog, you are always welcome to mine at **http://thebestparts.net**. A picture is worth a thousand words. And if you do visit, be sure to leave a comment! :-)

The remainder of the book will take you through the steps leading to writing your first blog post on ***your very own blog!*** I will also include a few other chapters of information that will make your blogging fun and easy! Modern computer technologies have made this remarkably simple, especially if we break it down into small steps. Ready?... Let's go!

Envision Your Blog

Before anything else, you should have some idea of what you will be writing on your blog so you can then come up with the perfect title for it. The possibilities are endless. Your blog can be focused on a specific topic like hiking, or cameras, or life in your hometown, or your favorite hobby. Or it can be general, more like a journal or diary of your life experiences and observations. You might want to showcase your photos, writing or poetry. You might want to start a mommy blog, about your kids and family. The subject and content of your blog is completely open to your imagination!

Later, once you have established your blog, you can always change the focus of your writing. You can even change the title of the blog, but you can't change the URL, which is the blog's web address as you would type it into your browser. It is always best if the title of your blog and the URL are the same. So it is important to take your time and give this some thought at the start. It might help to visit several, if not many blogs before you decide how you will want yours to be and what to name it. As a starting point, I might suggest visiting my blog, The Best Parts, at http://

thebestparts.net.

From there you can jump to other blogs by clicking on the links to some of my favorite blogs. You can find those links on my blog's sidebar (the column on the right) under "Blogroll."

Blogroll

- Rambling Stuff
- Tarheel Ramblings
- Berryvox
- Thoughtful Reflections
- San Diego Momma
- Counterfeit Humans
- Mike's Place
- The Kitchen Dispatch
- Mimi Writes
- Finding Pam
- Redhead Ranting
- Pregnant with Cancer
- Momma Mia, Mea Culpa
- Amalthy
- My Quality Day
- Gail Birdtale
- Elaine's Place
- Aurora's Tears
- Comedy Plus
- Shoes for an Imaginary Life
- The Junk Drawer

Many blogs will have a blogroll listing the favorite blogs of that particular author. In this way, you can jump from blog to blog, and you can get a good idea of the diversity of subjects and presentation. You will also get a good idea of the cool things you can do on a blog and the way people express their ideas.

After you have an idea of what you will be writing we can proceed with the next step, which is deciding on a name and tagline for your blog!

The Title and Tagline

So far…

- you have decided to start a blog.

- you have thought about the nature of your blog.

Now you will decide on the title/name of your blog, and on the tagline that goes along with it. For example, the title/name of my blog is "The Best Parts," and the tagline is "Fostering an attitude of gratitude." If you were to read some of the content on my blog you would see that it is a personal blog, about the good things in my life, for which I am grateful. As you have noticed on other blogs, the title and the tagline complement each other and give you a good idea of what you might find on that blog.

So first think about and decide on the title/name you will give your blog. It can be a short phrase or somewhat long. But keep in mind that the name of your blog will be part of the web address, also called the URL. That's the name you type into the browser to get to your blog. For example, notice how the name of my blog, "The Best Parts," translates into its URL: **http://thebestparts.net**.

Having a shorter name gives you a shorter URL. A longer one is okay, but you will be writing that URL on various forms for a long time, so the shorter the better, IMHO (in my humble opinion.)

The name of the blog should accurately reflect what the content will be. Hopefully, you can think of a clever name that will easily stick in readers' minds. In that sense, it is your first marketing effort to attract the right readers to your site.

Once you have decided on the title/name of your blog, next you should come up with several short phrases as candidates for your tagline. The tagline serves to further identify the nature of your blog. A good tagline will have a feeling to it. And it doesn't have to be sugar sweet. Many are clever and funny. I have even seen angry and sad taglines with good merit. It's the honesty and integrity that matter most. As much as possible, your blog posts (your writings) should mirror the name and tagline, though this is not at all a requirement.

Keep playing with the name and tagline until you find the combination that is just right!

BTW (by the way,) you noticed I said to keep "playing" with the name and tagline. This is very important! Blogging should be fun! Each step along the way, even if it is tricky at times, is part of the creative process. And in blogging, the creativity never stops. A blog site is always a work in progress. That is a big part of the fun! Take your time and be sure to enjoy each step along the way! There is no rush to any of this. Your blog will be up and running in no time anyway! :D

Blogging is fun! :-)

Choosing a Blogging Platform

So far…

- you have decided to start a blog.

- you have thought about the nature of your blog.

- you have decided on a name and tagline for your blog.

Now don't let the words "blogging platform" intimidate you. They simply refer to the fact that there are several systems out there for producing and publishing blogs. You can do a simple search for "blogging platforms" to get an idea of the various systems people use to write their blogs. They vary in ease of setup, ease of use, features and cost. WordPress and Blogger are the most commonly used systems for bloggers. I'll limit my initial comments to only those, and later will focus on WordPress (as you might have guessed from the title of this book! LOL)

I suggest you visit both of these sites to explore their options. http://wordpress.com and http://blogger.com/features. In particular, learn about setup and ease of use, as well as the variety of themes and plugins. (More on that later!) You should feel free to sign up for a free account at one or both of these sites, but I suggest you do not actually start a blog at this point. You should wait to consider the material in the next chapter before making the final choice.

You might want to make another visit to the blogosphere to see blogs written on both of these platforms. You can tell the ones written using WordPress in two ways. They will either have a URL with the word "wordpress" in it, e.g., http://blogname.wordpress.com, or, if you scroll down to the very bottom of a blog, in the footer area you will see something like "Powered by WordPress."

You can tell the blogs written using Blogger by finding the word "blogger" or "blogspot" in the URL, e.g., http://blogname.blogspot.com.

You'll see that both the WordPress and the Blogger platforms can produce very attractive blogs, and they are both easy to use.

Explore and learn about other platforms if you wish.

Once you have learned all that you want, make a decision on which platform you want to use. Fun! You're getting closer to starting your very own blog!

Hosted vs Self Hosted Blogs

So far…

- you have decided to start a blog.

- you have thought about the nature of your blog.

- you have decided on a name and tagline for your blog.

- you have chosen a blogging platform.

One last thing to consider before starting to set up the blog is whether you will have your blog files hosted for free at the sponsoring company's servers, or have your blog files self hosted by a provider of your own choosing and at your own cost.

You might be asking, "Why should I pay for hosting when I can get it for free?" Obviously, you get what you pay for. Having a free blog is fine. It really is. There are literally tens of millions of free blogs out there. But there are some limitations. All Blogger blogs are free. It is a way for Google, the owner of the Blogger platform, to bring you into their fold, with subtle encouragement to use other

Google services. But Blogger is popular because it is very easy to use, and there are plenty of theme and plugin options to make a blog attractive and functional.

Similarly, WordPress offers a free blog, hosted on the WordPress.com servers. They also have a wide variety of themes and plugins, though the options are limited compared to the WordPress option that is self hosted.

Self hosting gives you **ownership** of your blog and more control. It gives you more options for themes and plugins, which are used to give your blog the look and feel that you want and provide all manner of functionality. Self hosted blogs are easier to find by search engines. But perhaps more than anything, when you self host you actually **own your blog.** You pay for it. It is your very own little piece of the World Wide Web. And there is no one (like Google, e.g.) to potentially censor you.

On the surface your URL would look like this:

If hosted for free on a sponsor company: http://yourblogname.wordpress.com or http://yourblogname.blogspot.com. Notice the name of the sponsoring company complicates your URL.

If self hosting **your own blog**: http://yourblogname.com.

Most people would prefer to own a "dot com." Of course, you can purchase a ".net" or a ".me" or some other suitable suffix. I happen to own a ".net." Owning your own website is easy. There are many companies that will search for the availability of a certain domain name and sell you the exclusive right to it if it is available. Hopefully, the blog name you have chosen (which will be the domain name) has not already been chosen by anyone else in the world and is available for you to purchase. They are not expensive, usually about $10 per year. There is a definite pride and excitement that goes along with owning your own domain name!

I can be the owner and ruler of my own domain! :-)

If you choose to go the ownership route, you will also need to have your new domain hosted by one of many hosting companies. Web hosting would cost you about $8 per month. You can do a search for "domain names" and/or "web hosting" to get an idea of your many options. This is all easier than it sounds. Just keep reading.

Personally, I like to one-stop shop. For my blog named "The Best Parts," I purchased the domain name "thebestparts.net" and I have my site hosted by the same company. I chose **GoDaddy.com** because the prices for domain names and the fees for web hosting were competitive, and because of their reputation for excellent customer service, which includes the initial installation and setup of the WordPress files. As you might glean, ***I believe self hosted WordPress blogs, purchased and hosted on GoDaddy, is the way to go.*** But I will say that you would do just fine with a free blog on **Blogger.com** or **WordPress.com**, and that there are plenty of other domain name and web hosting companies out there if you choose to purchase your own domain name. In any case, if you choose to own your own site, you will have to decide on a domain name seller and a web hosting company.

BTW, this is a good time to mention that none of the fine companies I mention in this book are paying me anything for writing this book.

Create Your Blog!

So far…

- you have decided to start a blog.

- you have thought about the nature of your blog.

- you have decided on a name and tagline for your blog.

- you have chosen a blogging platform.

- you have decided between a hosted and a self hosted blog.

That means you are now ready to create your blog!

If you have chosen to start a free blog hosted on **WordPress.com**, it is as simple as clicking the orange "Get Started" button on the **WordPress.com** site. Simply follow the clear instructions and you will have a **WordPress.com** blog before you know it. After that, you will spend hours of fun trying out the various themes that will give your blog the look and feel you want. (More on themes and plugins later.) Remember, though you will have plenty of choices for themes and plugins, the options are greatly limited compared to having your own, self hosted WordPress blog.

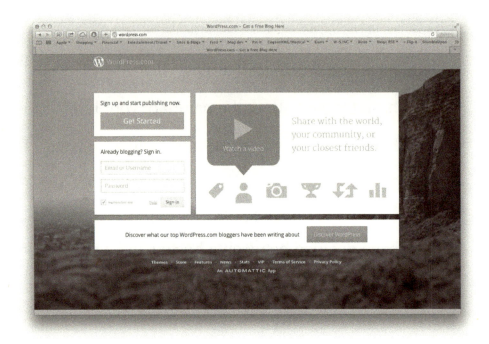

If you have chosen to start a free Blogger blog, it is as simple as clicking the orange "Get Started" button on the **blogger.com/features** page. Again, simply follow the step by step directions and you will soon be having the same fun with themes and plugins.

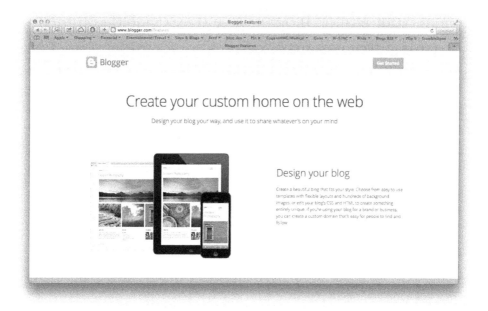

These free blogs are very simple to set up and use. They are almost self explanatory. Sure, a newbie will have questions. Both WordPress and Blogger have easy sources of information and answers. But if you were to need help, look for the help and support links. Look for member forums where people can ask and answer questions. Look for FAQ's (frequently asked questions.) Also, you can do a Google search for a specific question, or find a YouTube tutorial video. There are many ways to find answers to any question you may have about starting your blog.

I'll mention one last thing about free blogs on WordPress and Blogger. You can, at a later date, transfer all your blog content (your written blog posts and associated comments) to a domain that you may decide to purchase at some time in the future. It's a bit of a hassle but it can be done. This might help the frugal ones among you who don't want to shell out money at this time.

If you have decided to purchase **your own blog** name now, I congratulate you! You will have a slightly more complicated setup, which I will describe shortly. You will pay a total of about $100 a year. This includes the registration of your very own domain name and the "monthly" web hosting charge, which is usually charged at least one year at a time. And in return you will have total control of your blog, a huge assortment of themes and plugins with which to build your blog, better visibility for search engines, and a cool name with a simple dot com, dot net, etc.

Free is good.
You get what you pay for!
Hmm

The first thing you will do is to purchase your domain name, which is the name of your blog, from a vendor. Remember, I use GoDaddy.com but you can use any domain name vendor you'd like. They all have a search box to see if the name you have chosen for your blog is available. Type in that name and click search. For example, I typed in "the best parts." The search will instantly tell you if your desired name is available. If someone else already owns the name you type in, you will have to think of another name and its associated tagline. But hopefully your first choice will be available for you. You will see your blog name along with choices of internet suffixes such as .com, .net, .org, .me, .gov and others that are available. Each may have a slightly different price. I suggest you use either .com, .net, or .me for your blog. If you are satisfied, choose it, pay for it, and it is yours! This is a big moment!! It's okay to get all excited!!!

You are now the proud owner of your very own web site name! You will now need to have this new domain name hosted by a web hosting company. Again, remember that I use <u>GoDaddy.com</u> for this also. It is very simple to use the same vendor for both purchasing a domain name and for hosting it. When you have decided on your web hosting vendor, sign up with your new domain name, and you now have a web site! It is empty at this point, but it is your web site nevertheless and it will soon house your blog! And it wasn't that hard, was it!?

The final stage is to install the WordPress files into this new web site so that you can start to work on the look and feel of your blog, and to start blogging! One final reminder and I'll shut up about GoDaddy. Remember that I like to use them because they have very good customer service and the initial installation of the WordPress files is included with your web hosting package. I have always found the customer service people to be very helpful. Call them on the phone (YES, on the phone!) and they will walk you through the WordPress installation.

And that's it! You now have your very own web site and are ready to choose a theme, some plugins, and start blogging! Congratulations!!

From this point forward, I will focus on creating blogs using the self hosted WordPress platform. However, the concepts easily apply to all other blog writing systems.

Themes

Now that you are all set up, it is time to start designing the look and feel of your blog. Whether you will be using a free or a self hosted blog, whether you will be using WordPress, Blogger or any other platform, you will design your blog by using themes and plugins.

Before talking about themes and plugins, let me say a few words about how you will access them. Your blog platform will have an administration (admin) page, sometimes called an administration panel, or dashboard. WordPress calls it the "Dashboard." During the setup and installation of your blog, you will have been given a link to your sign in page. It looks like this:

Also during the setup and installation of your blog, you will have set up a name and password to sign in to the admin page. Enter the name and password and you are taken to your admin page, the WordPress Dashboard. It looks like this:

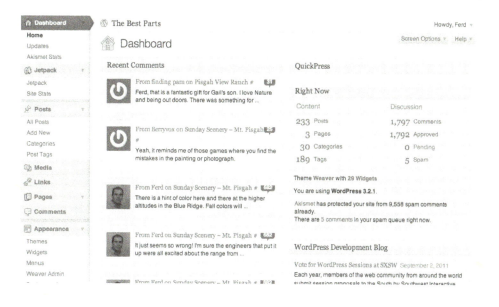

Take some time to look around. Here is where all the creativity takes place. From this panel you will search and choose your themes and plugins, write the actual posts, and manage all aspects of your blog!

So now let's talk about themes. A theme comprises the main look of the blog. As you have surfed the web, looking at other people's blogs, you have noticed a large variety of color schemes, headers, columns for writing, columns for sidebars, comment areas and footers. The variety is endless. Each one gives a character to the blog. Many smart nerds out there wrote all the computer code for these themes and this code is available for you to use to design your own blog. You don't ever have to write any code yourself! You will explore the huge variety of themes available to you, and eventually decide on the one that best portrays your personality and your writing style. Many of these themes are customizable so you can tweak colors, fonts, sizes, column widths, etc.

Here's how you do it. The column on the left side of the WordPress Dashboard is a menu of control items. About half way down you will see the "Appearance" control. Click the little triangle just to the right of the word "Appearance." It opens up the submenu. There you will find the link for "Themes." Clicking on it takes you to the theme management area.

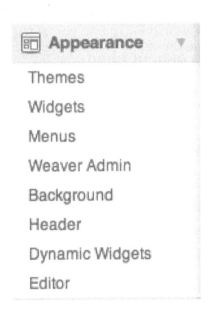

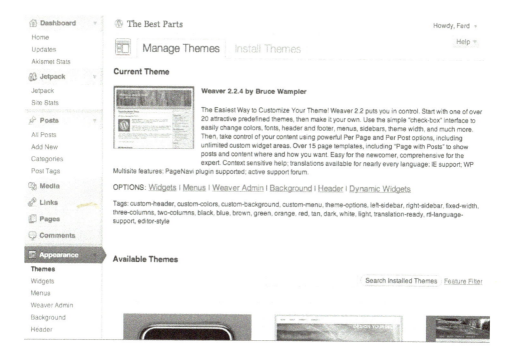

From now on in this book, a series of menu options such as "Appearance" followed by "Themes" will be represented as **Appearance>Themes**.

You will notice two items on the very top tabs: "Manage Themes" and "Install Themes." In the "Manage Themes" area, you will find the themes that are presently installed. When you install themes, they will appear in this area. Only one theme will be active at any one time. It is the very first one pictured, called the "Current Theme." If there is no "Current Theme," look for the theme called "Twenty Twelve" and click on the "Activate" link at the bottom of the description.

At this point, your blog is "live" on the Internet! It is visible to the whole world! You can visit your site and see what you have so far. If you type the name of your blog in any browser on any computer, you will now see your blog with the theme you have selected. Go ahead and check it out now. WordPress makes this even easier. At the very top of any Dashboard menu you will see the name of your blog. It is a link. Click on the name of your blog and you will be taken directly to it to see how things might have changed. You can then press your browser's "back button" to return to your Dashboard.

Now click on the other tab at the very top, the one that says "Install Themes." This is the time to have fun looking around and installing one or two, or two hundred themes! Use the search box or the feature filter. Try checking one or several boxes on the feature filter to see the themes with those characteristics. When you do, you will be able to "Preview" what the theme looks like. If you don't like it, you simply keep searching and previewing.

When you find a theme that you might like, go ahead and "Install" it. It will then appear in the "Manage Themes" tab along with the other themes that were already there. From the "Manage Themes" area you can "Preview" what your blog will actually look like, with your blog name and tagline already on it! If you still like it, you can "Activate" it.

You now know that when you install and activate a certain theme, you are never committed to keeping it forever. If you install and activate a different theme, it overwrites the previous one. Even later, after you have written many posts, you can always switch themes. Your old posts and the associated comments will magically appear on whatever new theme you choose. Remember, all of this is fun! And for most of us bloggers, gradually changing the look and feel of our blogs is an ongoing thing. Our blogs are a living "work in progress!"

After you have chosen a theme, explore the options you have for customizing it. If there are options, you will find a new link on the Dashboard's control menus with the name of your theme, usually in the "Appearance" or the "Settings" menus. Some themes are highly customizable and others are not at all. In the following screenshot, I am using the theme called "Weaver," and you will see a number of items on the control menus that allow me to customize this theme. In fact, that's why I chose this theme, because I like to be able to tweak and personalize the appearance of my blog.

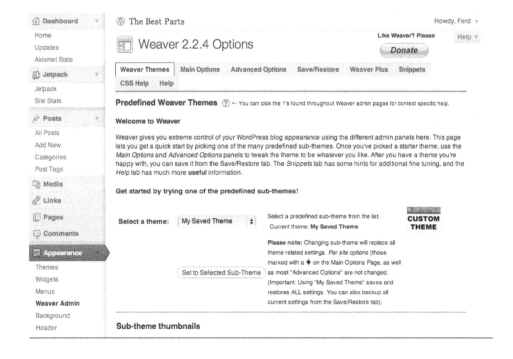

Once you are satisfied with the first look of your blog, it is time to write your first post. Wow! This is it! :-)

Your First Post

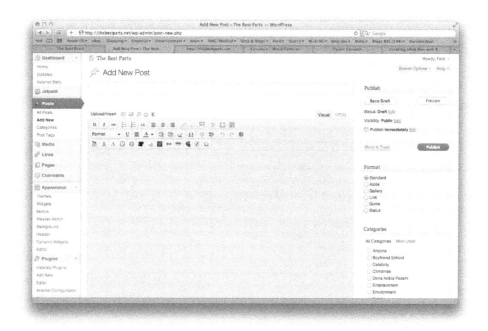

From the WordPress Dashboard choose **Posts>Add New**. This takes you to a window that is used for writing and editing your posts. This is a good time to explore how it works. Let's write a sample post that you can either edit or delete later. When you first open the "Add New Post" page, the cursor will be in the area for writing the title of the post. Go ahead and give this post a title, like "My first post" or any other title you prefer. Good! Now just below this area you will find a series of icons for the editing options that you can use to enhance your posts. They are intuitive and you can explore and use them later. Just below those icon links you will find a blank area. This is the "white space" where you will write your post. Click your cursor into this area. Now, write something. Use this first post just for practice. You can either edit it or completely delete it later. If you wish, try out the editing options. They are similar to any word processor you have used. There are also icons for adding other media items to your posts. More on that later.

In WordPress, when you look at your blog for the first time you will notice that there is already a sample post on it, provided by WordPress, entitled "Hello World." It is simply an example of a post, and it has a sample comment. You can edit this post, give it a different title, delete it, or you can keep it on your blog for posterity, as it marks the birthday of your blog! There is an upcoming chapter on editing and deleting.

When you finish your practice post, you may want to assign a category to it, and maybe a tag. These are optional. Categories and tags will be useful for searching through your blog in the future. At some point you will have dozens and hundreds of posts. You will probably have written about a number of different subjects. So think of a category to which your first post can belong. It might be something like "Blogging Stuff." Look for the area on the right sidebar where categories are created, then create it, and assign it to your post by checking the box.

Similarly, a tag is a one-word or very-short-phrase description of a particular something in your post. Think of tags as "key words." Again, they will be useful later, when you or a reader may want to search for items on your blog. Find the area where tags are assigned for this post and write one in if you'd like.

In case you haven't figured it out already, I will show you how to add pictures and other media to your posts in a later chapter. That will be very important because images add visual appeal and interest to your writing.

And that's it! Find the "Publish" button on the upper right hand side and press it! You have now published your first blog post. Congratulations! Go to your blog and see what it looks like. If you like it, leave it there. If not, you can later go back to your Dashboard and edit or delete it, but not until you read the next chapter about comments.

Comments

After you write your first post, you will wonder when or if anyone will ever see it. You will wonder how anyone even knows it's there. If you are like most people, you will want people to read what you wrote and to leave a comment. Blogging is not just about writing. It is about sharing your writing with an audience, and over time, developing a regular readership. The joy comes when these cyberspace visitors become eFriends, and a sense of community develops.

So how do comments work? When you go to your blog, like anyone in the world might go to your blog, you will see your written post, and at the bottom of the post you will find an area to leave a comment. Anyone can write in these text boxes to leave a comment. Go ahead and leave yourself a comment so you see what your readers will do when they visit your site.

As the owner of your blog, you have full control over how the comment process occurs. Maybe you want to review comments before they actually appear on your blog. Some people like to screen comments to be sure they are appropriate. Examine the **Settings>Discussion** area on the

Dashboard, where you can make certain choices about comments or discussion. Personally, I don't like to review comments before they appear. I think readers who take the time to leave a comment like to see their comment appear on the blog right away, not having to wait until you approve the comment at some later time. Inappropriate comments can always be deleted later, from the Dashboard of course. There are also other ways to prevent unwanted comments. You will learn more about managing comments in the "Editing and Deleting" chapter to follow.

Attracting readers to your blog, readers who will hopefully comment on what you have written, is such an important topic it deserves its own chapter. Read on!

Finding Interested Readers

Once you have written a blog post, you will likely be looking forward to having it read by people who will visit your blog. More than that, you will appreciate their written comments. And later, when you encounter people who see the world on similar terms, you will enjoy their repeated visits and comments. That will be the beginning of your "community" within the blogosphere!

You are probably asking yourself, "How does that happen?"

The answer is simple. You have to visit other people's blogs, read their stuff, and leave comments. Let me repeat that for emphasis. *Visit other blogs and leave comments!* As much as possible, when you visit other blogs, take a little time to leave a comment. The first time you do, you will probably have to register your name, email address, and your blog's URL. After you do that, the writer of the blog you visited will likely return the favor and visit yours, and other readers of that blog can easily click on your name and be linked directly to your blog. You will get readers/commenters if you become a reader/commenter yourself. That is how communities develop!

If you have never done this before, there are two good ways to search for blogs that are interesting to you. One I already mentioned. Start at anyone's blog, mine for instance (http://thebestparts.net) and click on one of my blogroll links in the sidebar. You will be taken to that blog, and they will likely have a blogroll, too. In that way, you can jump from blog to blog, and gradually find blogs that you like for one reason or another. I will later discuss ways to keep track of these blogs so you can visit them again in the future. If you really like a blog, you might become "a regular."

The other good way to search for blogs is through the large blog directories, where literally millions of blogs are registered. In fact, it is a good idea for you to register your blog, too, so others can find yours! I suggest you register your blog at the largest blog directory, BlogCatalog.com. From there, anyone can do a search for a particular topic of interest and find many blogs that fit the description. You can easily begin your explorations there.

As you can see, blogging is about writing, reading, sharing, commenting, and interacting. It is a way to develop meaningful relationships with like minded people that are physically scattered all over the world. It all starts with the writing and the comments, and it goes both ways.

45

Editing and Deleting

In WordPress, the editing and deleting functions work similarly for posts and for comments.

After a post has been written and published, you may want to change (edit) the post in some way. WordPress makes that easy to do. From the Dashboard, choose **Posts>All Posts**. The next window shows a listing of all the posts that have ever been written on your blog. If you hover the cursor over the title of a post, several options will appear under the title, including View, Edit and Trash.

Find the post you used as a sample for practice. Hover the cursor over the title so the options appear. Choose Edit. You will see that this takes you back to the same writing window you used to write the post in the first place. You can then make changes to your post. Try changing a few things. Add to, delete, or change any of the content. After you have done so, click the "Update" button on the upper right hand side. And that's it! You can go to your blog to confirm that the changes took effect. You might need to refresh the screen.

If instead of editing you wish to delete the post

altogether, you can either use the "Move to Trash" link that you will see just to the left of the "Update" button, or you can choose the "Trash" link when you first hover your cursor over the title of the unwanted post in the "All Posts" list.

Editing and deleting comments works in just the same way. From the Dashboard, choose **Comments**. You will see a listing of all the comments people have left on your blog posts, starting with the most recent comment. Hover the cursor on any part of the comment listing and the comment management options appear just beneath the comment, including Unapprove (if already approved,) Approve (if you have chosen to review/approve comments before they appear on your blog,) Reply, Edit, Spam and Trash. I advise strongly against editing other people's comments, unless it is a simple typo and with the comment writer's permission. But it is your complete prerogative to Unapprove or Delete a comment at your discretion.

A little bit ago, I thought I heard you asking, "What the heck is Spam!?" No, it's not ham in a can. It's a lot worse than that! Spam is a sort of comment that comes from unscrupulous internet marketers. They are always looking for ways to sell a product. They are not interested in what you write, though the spam comment might make a lame attempt to address the content of your post. Spam comments usually have several links back to the site where their product is sold. Spam is a big nuisance. When a spam comment appears in your comments, it is good to mark it as spam and then to delete it. Use the appropriate comment management options to do that.

Fortunately, there are spam filters available for all blog platforms. In the WordPress world, the plugin called "Akismet" functions as a very effective spam filter, automatically recognizing, marking and deleting spam comments for you. It captures 99% of all spam comments. This plugin is a *must have!* More on plugins later.

Another way to ward off spam comments is to use a different kind of plugin generally called a "CAPTCHA." This is basically a short form that a commenter is required to fill out before the comment is accepted. The forms involve copying a series of random letters and numbers that are distorted in such a way that an automatic spam generator cannot recognize them. (Spammers are clever and use automatic programs to leave comments.) You will find many blogs using a CAPTCHA plugin like this. Personally, I hesitate to use one because it creates one extra step for a reader of my blog to leave a comment, and it might be just enough for that person to not leave the comment at all. I prefer to use Akismet to capture 99% of spam comments, and then to delete by hand the 1% that get through. I prefer to do this small task instead of asking my readers to do the CAPTCHA task. I like to promote an easy commenting experience on my blog.

Adding Pictures to Your Posts

Images can complement your writing and greatly enhance the beauty and readability of your blog posts. Writing on a blog is not like the writing you did for your teachers in school. Writing on a blog often includes the use of images in addition to your writing to better transmit your message. In fact, there are some blogs that focus on the photo instead of the writing. These are called photoblogs. And many people who blog will often participate in photography memes such as the popular "Wordless Wednesday," which as you probably gather, involves posting an interesting photo on Wednesdays, without words, sharing the image alone.

Ideally, these are pictures that you take yourself, though there are plenty of public domain images on the internet that anyone can use on their posts without infringing on copyrights. Your blogging platform, whether it's WordPress, Blogger, or anything else, makes it easy to add pictures to your posts. In fact, you will find it is easy to add music, videos, and an endless variety of third party content to your blog. The ability to use multimedia is what makes blogging different from just writing. And all this will make your posts more interesting and readable.

Maybe you are thinking this is all too complicated. I am pretty sure you will discover that it is not. You can be technologically challenged and still create a beautiful blog! You will likely find it interesting to learn something new. You will feel the thrill of discovering a new way of communicating your thoughts. You will develop your own style. You might discover new interests. And little by little you will create blog posts that are interesting and visually appealing. Your entire blog site will gradually become a beautiful place of which you can be proud.

A blog is like a home, where friends visit! :-)

So how do you add pictures to your posts? It is simple. Again, I am focusing on WordPress, but other systems will have a very similar approach.

As you write a new post in the writing/editing window, look above the writing/editing window to see rows of little editing icons. As you hover your cursor over the little icons, words appear to describe their functions. On the top row, find the larger editing button that says "Add Media." When you click this icon, a new window appears. In this window you can drag and drop an image from your desktop, or you can "Select Files."

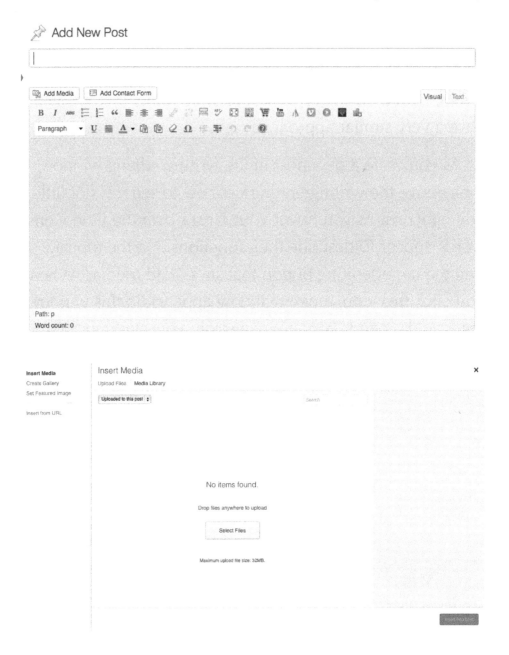

Click the "Select Files" button and navigate to your

image. Of course, you should have an image on your computer that you intend to use. When you find and select that image, it will be uploaded to WordPress. After the upload completes, another window appears with various choices on how you will want that image to appear in your post. Take a look at each of the choices. For now, leave all the choices as they are already set. Go to the bottom of that window and click on "Insert into post." Now, when you go back to the writing/editing window, you will see your picture! You will learn to place your picture at the beginning of the post, or anywhere in the body of the text, or at the end. You will see that you can make the picture small, medium or large. You can place the picture on the left, right, or centered. You can give it a title. There are many ways for you to fashion your image so that it will appear just the way you want it on your post!

BTW, after you have uploaded an image to WordPress, it is saved on the WordPress server forever, unless you choose to delete it for some reason. You don't have to upload it again if you want to use that same image on a later post.

Images on blog posts make such a difference that you might find yourself carrying your camera everywhere you go! That's a very bloggy thing to do! :-)

More About Images

I decided to add this chapter to give you a little head start on the use of images on your blog.

Obviously, you will need a digital camera. These days, your phone may have a very good digital camera, and that would work just fine. But you may want to have a dedicated camera. If you don't already have one, there are many brands and hundreds of models to choose from. You will need to pick one based on your knowledge of cameras, features, cost, ease of use, etc. Any digital camera will have a way or ways for you to transfer the images to your computer.

Once your images are on your computer, you will want to organize them in some way. There are many photo organization programs out there. You will want to research them and pick one.

Photo organization programs frequently have simple photo editing capabilities as well. This is handy because you may want to do simple adjustments to your images, such as cropping and enhancing. As an alternative, you may want to have a dedicated photo editing program. These are more complicated, but allow you to do many more image adjustments. Your choices of camera, photo organization software, and possibly photo editing software, will depend on your knowledge of these things. As you continue blogging, you can bet that your knowledge will grow and grow because the use of images in your blog posts is so important. Images will personalize your site and greatly enhance the experience for you and for your readers.

In the previous chapter, I described how to add an image to a blog post. That is the simple mechanism included with WordPress, and it may be all you ever use. But you will see other bloggers display their images in creative ways that are not an essential part of WordPress. They do this through the use of plugins. To give you a quick, introductory look, go to your Dashboard and check out **Plugins>Add New**. At the bottom of the screen that follows you will find a list of "Popular tags." Click on the "images" tag to see hundreds of plugins that can add some sort of image functionality to any blog. In the next chapter, I will go into more detail about plugins, and special plugins called widgets.

Plugins and Widgets

Plugins and widgets are funny words that can sound really mysterious or even scary if you are technologically challenged. They are some of the building blocks of your blog, so it's important to know about them. Let's take the mysterious and scary out of them!

A plugin is a little program that has been written by someone else to add a certain function to your blog. There are thousands of these. Some of them are part of your blogging system from the start, and some you can add at any time if you wish. For example, you might add a plugin that links your post to Facebook or other social media. There are plugins that can enhance the way you display your images. Plugins can modify how comments are handled. They can make it easy to display certain things like music and video. These are just a few examples of what plugins can do for your blog.

Plugins are not necessary, but at some point you will want a certain feature on your blog that you have seen on other people's blogs. You will discover that they do it through a plugin. You will do a search for that plugin and install it on your site. How does this happen? Let me show you by way of example.

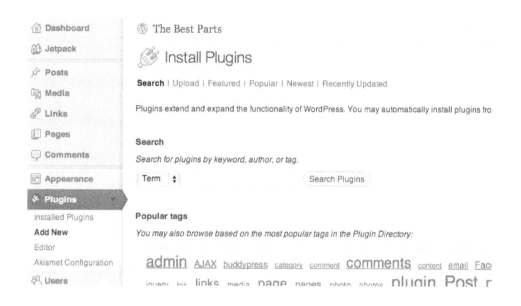

Let's add a plugin that allows you or your viewers to add your post to Facebook. From the WP Dashboard, click **Plugins>Add New**. The "Install Plugins" window appears. In the middle of the window is a search box. Type in the word "facebook" to search for all the plugins that have the word "facebook" in their title. You might be surprised at the results, with page after page of plugins that somehow add a way to add a Facebook function to your blog. On these pages you can read a summary of what each plugin will do for your blog, and if you're interested you can read more detail. You can see the ratings by current users and the number of people using that particular plugin. You can see if it is compatible with your version of WordPress. You can preview what it would look like on your blog without installing it. And when you find one you'd like to try, you simply click "Install." After it installs on your WordPress site, you then have to "activate" it. And that's it! The plugin and its functionality are installed on your site. If at any point you want to remove it, it is as simple as going to the Plugins area and clicking "deactivate." In this way, you can try one or many plugins and see how you like them.

If you have a Facebook account, you may want to choose one of these plugins and activate it. This kind of plugin usually automatically adds a little link button at the end of your posts. When a reader (including yourself) reads your post, they can click the Facebook button and a link to your blog post appears on their Facebook News Feed. Cool! BTW, adding your own blog posts to your own Facebook News Feed is an easy way to direct your Facebook friends to your blog!

Remember, you can always remove any plugin and its function at any time.

Widgets are plugins that add functionality in a more visible and active way. You can modify settings and make adjustments to a widget through some sort of control panel that is a part of the widget itself. In WordPress, sidebar elements are called "widgets."

To add a widget to your blog's sidebar, go to the dashboard and click **Appearance>Widgets**. Examine the window which is now displayed.

On the left side are your "Available Widgets." The right hand column represents your blog's sidebar and other widget areas. This right hand column may look different, depending on which WordPress theme you are using. You will see a series of tabs with the different locations available for widgets. Go ahead and experiment with the these tabs. Click on the little triangle to the right of the tab titles to open and close their windows.

Now locate the tab which is the primary widget area for your sidebar, and click the little triangle to the right of the title, which opens up its window. Leave the window open. Now look to the group of available widgets on the left and locate the one that says "Recent Posts." Drag this button to the right and drop it into the little window you just left open. The widget window now opens up automatically so you can see the available control options for this widget. Let's set this widget up. You may leave the "Title:" field blank. If you do so, the widget will retain the title "Recent Posts" when seen in your sidebar. If you prefer a different title for this widget, then write it into the "Title:" field. The next option is the number of posts to show. Write a number from 5 to 10, though you may show as many posts as you'd like on your sidebar. The final option is a check box, "Display post date?" Click on it if you'd like to see the post date as well as the post title on your sidebar. And that's it! If you now go to your blog, you will see you have a sidebar widget named "Recent Posts" with your most recent posts. It will automatically refresh as you write more posts. All widgets work more or less this way. New widget choices can be added to your available widget area by downloading their plugin. If there is a certain functionality you want to add to your blog's sidebar, do a plugin search for it and you're likely to find suitable options.

And now you know a little about plugins and widgets!

RSS Feeds

Writing on your blog makes you a publisher! Imagine that you are a writer for a newspaper. Your written articles would be published in the newspaper, which would then be distributed around the city so that many people could read it. Now think of your blog in exactly the same way. I'm sure you have noticed that when you have finished writing an article, you click a button that says "Publish" to post it on your blog. Your written blog posts are "published" on your blog, and they are essentially distributed all over the world for many people to read. In fact, your blog has the potential to reach many more readers than a local newspaper can.

Back to our newspaper analogy. Readers can "subscribe" to their local newspaper. They would do that if they value the content or the convenience of home delivery. Similarly, people who value the content of your blog can subscribe to it, so they can receive a copy of your blog posts as soon as they are published.

We can also make an analogy to radio or TV programming. The producers of radio and TV shows want their programs to be seen by as many people as possible. So they sell rights to their programs to as many individual stations as possible. This is called syndication. The producers of the programs then provide a "feed" to the subscribing stations so they can then transmit the program to their customers.

Subscribing and syndication are possible in the blog world because WordPress and all other blog platforms can generate the content of your blog in different ways. One way is what you can see on the internet using normal web browsers like Safari, Firefox, Chrome, Internet Explorer and others. Another way is to generate the content of your blog, lets call it a "feed," in a way that can be read by electronic readers specifically designed to capture this feed and display it on a computer. This system is called RSS, which stands for "Real Simple Syndication!"

WordPress produces a RSS feeds for your blog posts. People who like your blog may want to follow your posts using their favorite RSS reader. There are many such RSS readers. You can do a Google search for RSS readers to explore the various readers that are available. I use the RSS reader function on my free **WordPress.com** account. Again, the reason to use this feature, if you want to, is to be immediately notified when a new post has been published on one of your favorite blogs. Some people follow dozens of blogs, so following them by their RSS feed is more time efficient. You only visit the ones that have published new content. You can bet that some people will be following your blog in this way. Hopefully, many people! :-)

Most RSS readers will find a blog's RSS feeds automatically. If you want to follow a certain blog's posts, you just add the URL of that blog into the reader and it will find the RSS feeds for you.

There is a lot more to learn about RSS feeds, but you at least now have a basic understanding of what RSS feeds are all about. If you want to learn more about WordPress RSS feeds, check **here**.

Statistics

Bloggers like to know how many people are visiting their blogs. Most visitors do not leave comments, so the comment count is not an accurate measure of how many people have visited. But there are easy ways to obtain this interesting information. You will have to choose and install a statistics plugin, also known as a statistics program or package.

WordPress now comes with a preinstalled package of enhancements called "Jetpack." You can find the link to it just underneath the Dashboard link on the WordPress control panel sidebar. If for some reason Jetpack is not present in your WordPress installation, do a plugin search for "Jetpack" and install/activate it. Included in this package is a basic statistics program. You will want to activate this very useful program as soon as possible. It will keep track of the number of readers, and other very useful information. You can see this information under **Jetpack>Site Stats**.

In addition to the WordPress Jetpack analytics, you may want to install a more robust statistics package.

If you are a Google user, it would be very easy to use Google Analytics. You can visit their main web page at **http://www.google.com/analytics** and sign up your blog.

There are many other statistics packages out there. You can do a WordPress plugin search for the word "statistics" or "stats" and you will see more than twenty pages of available plugins!

In addition to Jetpack, I also use a third party statistics package called "SiteMeter." Like so many other third party software programs available for blogs, SiteMeter has a fully functional free version, and a more comprehensive version that costs a little money per month. I am very happy using the free version. It gives me all the information I want, such as number of visits per day and number of pages viewed per visitor. The free version can also break this information down to greater detail. The paid version gives you even more information and detail. You can check this out at **http://sitemeter.com**.

If you decide to use SiteMeter, you will register your blog information, and they will generate the computer code that you must install into your blog so that SiteMeter can read the activity and report back to you. This computer code will be provided to you at **SiteMeter.com** as soon as you have registered your blog. You must copy that code and paste it into a Text widget somewhere on your blog. I will walk you through the steps of how to add HTML code to a WordPress Text widget in the next chapter, using SiteMeter as an example.

After you have installed it, the SiteMeter logo will appear where you have placed it. I placed mine in the Footer area.

After that, you can go to **SiteMeter.com** and examine up to the moment visitor activity on your blog!

Adding HTML Code to Widgets

To work with WordPress, you don't have to know anything about writing computer code. But it is important to know how to add bits of code to your blog when you want to add certain functions.

In the previous chapter we talked about the statistics program called "SiteMeter." In this chapter we will go over the process of signing up for a third party program such as SiteMeter, and specifically the part that has to do with installing the provided computer code into your blog.

The idea of a "third party" simply refers to a person/product/service that is different from you (the first party) and WordPress (the second party.) There are many (third party) individuals and companies that have developed programs that add a special function to WordPress. In fact, WordPress was designed specifically to promote these third party ideas. Some are available in the WordPress plugins section. Others like SiteMeter, are not available by way of a WordPress plugin, making them just a little bit trickier to install.

Go to **SiteMeter.com** and explore what this statistics

program is all about. You will see that there is a free version and a paid version. We will use the free version.

Next, go through the steps required to register your blog. You will be asked to provide the usual information such as your name, email address, your blog's URL, to establish a password, etc. At the completion of registration you will be shown a window with a gobbledygook of computer code. That is your unique code for a little program that will read visitor activity on your blog and report it back to SiteMeter. SiteMeter will then use that information to produce charts and graphs for you to know how many people visit your blog, what posts they read, how much time they spent on your blog, where they came from, and much more.

Copy the contents of the window that has the computer code. We will now paste it into your blog.

Go to your WordPress Dashboard and go to **Appearance>Widgets**. This will take you to the Widgets page. As you already know, the column on the right side is a representation of your sidebar and other widget areas. At the bottom of that column is an area for "Footer" widgets. Find the button that says "Footer" or "First Footer Area" and click it. It opens a little window. Leave it open.

Now on the left side of the Widgets page find the button that says "Text." Drag that Text button over to the little

"Footer" window which you just left open and drop it into that window. The Text window now opens. In the title area, write "SiteMeter." In the main area, paste the SiteMeter computer code which you had copied earlier. Now go down to the bottom of the little Text window and press "Save." And that's it! Go to your blog and scroll down to the bottom. In the footer area you should see the SiteMeter logo, right where you placed it!

You have now installed the SiteMeter code into your blog. It will start capturing visitor information and report it back to SiteMeter. You will be able to access that information on the SiteMeter site using your SiteMeter name and password.

If for some reason in the future you want to remove the SiteMeter function, it is as easy as removing that Text widget from the Footer area of the Widgets page. You simply drag it back over to the left hand side of the Widgets page.

Many other third party programs are installed in the exact same way. Now you know how to add computer code to your blog, by way of a Text widget onto your Sidebar or Footer areas!

Final Thoughts and Credits

I want to thank you very much for buying this book. Many technical books have been written about blogging. The idea behind *this* one was to help make the process of starting and owning your own blog *easy!* I hope you have found it to be just that. Certainly there is much more to learn than what was covered here, but you should now know more than enough to have your blog up and running. You will surely learn more as you blog on!

I sincerely hope you find joy in your blogging and good companionship in the wonderful community of bloggers.

Credits

Many thanks to my daughter, Ginny Crotte, for her valuable insights, advice, encouragement and editing as I was writing this book.

About the Author

Ferd Crotte is your average middle-aged Internal Medicine hospitalist enjoying life in the Great State of North Carolina. His many interests include blogging, starting with the off-beat **Crazy Medical Cases** and then The Best Parts for the past eight years. By email, he helped a friend start her own blog. The step by step instructions turned into this ebook!

Drawing on the experience of writing this first book, Ferd is now writing, under his professional name **Fernando Crotte, M.D.**, a medical series covering topics of common interest. For more information and to be added to the mailing list, visit…

The Understanding Series **website**

The Understanding Series **Facebook page**

You can find issues of **The Understanding Series** on…

Amazon

Barnes & Noble

The Sony Reader Store

Apple iBookstore

Smashwords

Lulu